Ver

NORTH DAKOTA

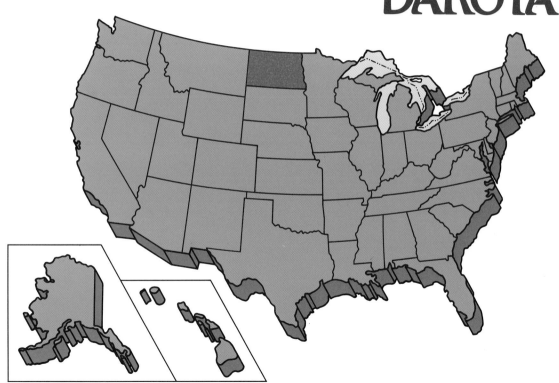

Hello U.S.A.

NORTH DAKOTA

Joan Marie Verba

Lerner Publications Company

LIBRARY OF CONGRESS
CATALOGING-IN-PUBLICATION DATA
Verba, Joan Marie.
     North Dakota / Joan Marie Verba.
         p.   cm. — (Hello USA)
     Includes index.
     Summary: An introduction to the geography, history, economy, people, environmental issues, and interesting sites of North Dakota.
     ISBN 0-8225-2746-4 (lib. bdg.)
     1. North Dakota—Juvenile literature.
[1. North Dakota.] I. Title. II. Series.
F636.3.V47   1992
978.4—dc20   91–40639
                              CIP
                              AC

Cover photograph by Lynda Richards.

The glossary on page 69 gives definitions of words shown in **bold type** in the text.

Manufactured in the United States of America

1 2 3 4 5 6 98 97 96 95 94 93

 This book is printed on acid-free, recyclable paper.

CONTENTS

Did You Know . . . ?

☐ Jamestown, North Dakota, is home to the World's Largest Buffalo. The statue, which stands on a hilltop, weighs 60 tons (54 metric tons).

☐ The geographic center of the North American continent lies near a town called Rugby, North Dakota, 45 miles (72 kilometers) south of the Canadian border.

☐ More ducks make their nests in North Dakota than in any other state except Alaska.

☐ Sometimes, when lightning strikes or when dry prairie grasses catch fire in the Badlands of North Dakota, the ground cracks open and the coal underneath catches fire. The coal can burn for many years, hardening the ground and turning it brick red.

☐ The International Peace Garden near Dunseith, North Dakota, lies partly in the United States and partly in Canada. The flowers and trees in the park stand for the long friendship between the two countries.

A Trip Around the State

Some people think of North Dakota as an empty, flat land. But those who get to know the state discover that it offers scenic lakes and rivers, rolling hills, and colorful plant and animal life. North Dakota is a midwestern state, lying between Canada to the north and South Dakota directly to the south. On the east, the Red River separates North Dakota from Minnesota. To the west is Montana.

Three geographic regions define the land of North Dakota. The Red River Valley stretches along the state's eastern border. The Drift Prairie runs north to south through the middle of the state, and the Missouri Plateau spreads over most of western North Dakota.

9

Potholes (small lakes) often dry up when it is hot but fill up again after a heavy rain.

A giant lake called Agassiz once covered the Red River Valley region. The lake was formed when **glaciers,** enormous, slow-moving sheets of ice, carved a huge hollow in the ground during the last **Ice Age.** Water from melting glaciers and from nearby rivers filled up the giant hollow. The lake dried up thousands of years ago, leaving flat land and rich soil behind. North Dakota's farmers now plant crops in the Red River Valley.

The Drift Prairie is pothole country. As glaciers passed over this region, they scooped out thousands of small, shallow basins. Rain then filled them up, creating little lakes known as **potholes.**

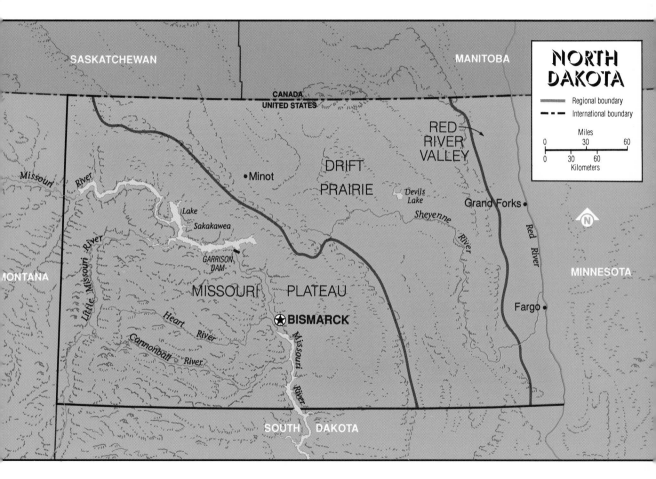

SASKATCHEWAN

MANITOBA

CANADA
UNITED STATES

NORTH DAKOTA

Regional boundary
International boundary

Miles
0   30   60

0   30   60
Kilometers

N

Missouri   River

• Minot

DRIFT
PRAIRIE

RED
RIVER
VALLEY

Devils
Lake

Grand Forks •

Red River

MONTANA

Little   Missouri   River

Lake
Sakakawea

GARRISON
DAM

MISSOURI   PLATEAU

★ BISMARCK

Heart   River

Cannonball   River

Sheyenne   River

MINNESOTA

Missouri   River

Fargo •

SOUTH   DAKOTA

Most of the Drift Prairie region is **prairie**, or grassland. The prairie soil is very rich. When the glaciers melted, they left behind thick layers of **drift**, a mixture of clay, sand, and gravel, which made good dirt.

Much of North Dakota's wheat is grown on the Drift Prairie.

The Missouri Plateau is part of a **plateau** (highland) called the Great Plains, which stretches all the way from Canada to Texas. North Dakota's ranchers graze their cattle on the grasslands of the Missouri Plateau. Workers also mine the rich deposits of oil and coal that lie underneath the ground in this region.

In the southwestern part of the Missouri Plateau are the lonely **buttes,** or isolated hills, of the Badlands. Wind and water have carved these rocky hills into unusual shapes. Minerals in the rock add colorful bands of brown, red, and yellow to the buttes.

Not all of North Dakota is flat. The colorful hills of the Badlands *(above)* attract many visitors. The western part of the state, where the Killdeer Mountains rise *(facing page)*, is good for ranching.

Winter frost outlines trees and grasses along the Missouri River.

The Missouri River—the second-longest river in the United States—winds its way south across western North Dakota. The river is sometimes called Big Muddy because of all the mud in its water. The Little Missouri, Heart, and Cannonball rivers flow into the Missouri River.

Along the state's eastern border, the Red River heads north into Canada. The Sheyenne and several smaller rivers drain into the Red River.

Devils Lake is the largest natural lake in the state. But Lake Sakakawea, an artificial lake, is bigger. It was formed when the Garrison Dam was built to collect floodwaters on the Missouri River.

Long, cold winters and short, hot summers are common in North Dakota. Wind blows blizzards into the state in the winter and brings heat waves in the summer. Temperatures average 70° F (21° C) in summer and only 7° F (–14° C) in winter. During the winter, the state gets about 32 inches (81 centimeters) of snow.

North Dakota is one of the driest states in the country. Some western areas of the state receive only about 13 inches (33 cm) of **precipitation** (rain and melted snow) each year. Farmers in the eastern part of the state, though, can usually count on getting about 20 inches (51 cm).

Because of the dry weather, North Dakota does not have many trees. Only about 1 percent of the land is forested, mostly with aspen, poplar, white pine, cedar, and cottonwood. In spring and summer, the prairie comes alive with the bright blossoms of pasqueflowers, coneflowers, and red lilies. Chokecherries, highbush cranberries, and wild plums ripen on the grasslands.

White-tailed deer roam throughout the state. In the Badlands, prairie dogs dig their underground homes, and mule deer and pronghorn antelope leap among the rocks and crags. One of North Dakota's nicknames—the Flickertail State—comes from the flickertail squirrels that make their homes in the central part of the state.

Huge herds of bison, or buffalo, once grazed on North Dakota's prairie, but millions were killed by hunters in the 1800s. The U.S. government then passed laws to protect bison. About 15,000 buffalo now live in game preserves, parks, and on private ranches.

North Dakota's Story

The first people to live in what is now North Dakota were hunters. They came to the area more than 10,000 years ago, when glaciers still covered most of North America. The hunters probably crossed a land bridge, which once connected Asia to North America, while they were stalking animals such as mammoths—huge creatures that looked like hairy elephants. The descendants of these hunters, called Indians or Native Americans, eventually settled throughout North America.

Around the year 400 B.C., groups of people moved to North Dakota from the forests of what are now Minnesota and Wisconsin. Now called Woodland Indians, these people lived in villages along the rivers of eastern North Dakota and built houses of branches, grasses, bark, and hides. The Woodland Indians hunted deer and buffalo and grew corn and squash.

For thousands of years, Native Americans hunted buffalo by chasing them off cliffs called buffalo jumps. After tumbling over the edge of these cliffs, the animals lay injured on the ground below. The hunters then went to the bottom of the cliffs, where they could easily kill and butcher their prey.

After A.D. 600, hunters began to follow herds of buffalo across the plains of what is now western North Dakota. These hunters, who may have been descendants of earlier Woodland Indians, are known as Plains Indians. Always on the move, these Plains Indians lived in tepees, which were easy to put up and take down.

Other Plains Indians made more permanent homes near the Missouri River. Among these were the Mandan, who moved west from the Mississippi River valley in A.D. 1000 and settled along the Missouri River in what is now North Dakota. Later, the Hidatsa and Arikara settled near the Mandan.

Tepee rings—large circles of stones—held tepees in place.

Mandan women made boats called bullboats by stretching buffalo hides over willow frames. The buffalo's tail was left on to mark the back of a boat. A large bullboat could hold as many as eight people.

The Mandan, Hidatsa, and Arikara lived in permanent villages of earthen homes. As many as 1,200 people would live in a village surrounded by a ditch and a wall of wooden posts for protection. In nearby fields, residents grew corn, beans, squash, and sunflowers. These Indians also hunted buffalo, eating the meat and using the hides for clothes and the bones for tools.

The Dakota placed their dead on platforms above the ground to dry. The bones of the dead were later buried.

22

In about 1700, the Ojibway Indians drove their enemies, the Dakota, or Sioux, out of central Minnesota. The Dakota made new homes in the Drift Prairie region of what is now North Dakota. The state takes its name from these Indians. *Dakota* means "allies," or "friends," in their language.

The first European to visit what is now North Dakota was a French Canadian fur trader named Pierre de La Vérendrye. He walked from Canada to North Dakota in 1738, setting up fur-trading posts along the way. British, French, and Spanish fur traders soon followed.

These traders gave metal pots, glass beads, cloth, and guns to the Indians in exchange for buffalo hides and meat. White traders wanted beaver furs, too, which were popular in Europe for making hats.

The traders also carried diseases such as smallpox, cholera, measles, and tuberculosis. Native Americans had never been exposed to these illnesses before, and thousands died.

La Vérendrye

23

In their search for furs and other riches, European nations gradually claimed much of the land on which Native Americans had made their homes for centuries. The French, for example, claimed a huge area that stretched all the way from the Mississippi River to the Rocky Mountains. Almost all of what is now North Dakota was part of this claim, called the Louisiana Territory. France sold the Louisiana Territory to the United States in 1803.

In the spring of 1804, U.S. president Thomas Jefferson sent explorers Meriwether Lewis and William Clark to map the new territory. Lewis and Clark traveled by canoe up the Missouri River from St. Louis, Missouri. In the fall, the explorers arrived at the villages of the Mandan and the Hidatsa and built Fort Mandan to live in until spring.

While at Fort Mandan, Lewis and Clark met Sakakawea, a young Shoshone Indian woman. In April 1805, Sakakawea joined the expedition. She guided the group and helped bring it safely to the Pacific Coast and back again.

Explorers Lewis and Clark met Sakakawea at the villages of the Mandan and the Hidatsa Indians.

In 1812 Thomas Douglas, a Scottish nobleman, brought a group of Scottish and Irish **immigrants** (newcomers) to North America. They settled near two important fur-trading posts in what is now the northeastern corner of North Dakota. The immigrants grew food for the trappers and traders. The immigrants' new town, Pembina, was North Dakota's first white settlement.

By 1830 North Dakota had many trading posts. Native Americans came with furs to Fort Union and Fort Clark on the Missouri River. Steamboats carried the furs down the river to St. Louis and returned with manufactured goods to be traded for more furs.

At Pembina, wagons known as Red River carts were loaded with buffalo robes and furs. Traders followed the Red River on their way to St. Paul, Minnesota, where they exchanged their goods for manufactured products.

Many pioneers traveled to what is now North Dakota to claim free land offered by the U.S. government. Settlers often made the journey in covered wagons.

As pioneers moved to the West, the U.S. government created territories out of the land they settled. A territory did not have as much power as a state, but with enough people, a territory could apply for statehood. In 1861 the U.S. government established the Dakota Territory. The territory included what are now North and South Dakota and much of Montana and Wyoming.

To encourage more white settlers to move to the new territory, the United States offered land for sale at very low prices. At first, few settlers came to the Dakota Territory because it was difficult to travel that far west. Trains did not go as far as the Dakota Territory. Travel by covered wagon was slow. On such a long journey across the isolated prairies, sickness and injury often meant death.

Many white people faced the dangers anyway. As white settlers moved farther and farther west, they forced Native Americans off the land. The U.S. government made treaties, or agreements, allowing Native Americans to keep some land. But the government often broke the treaties, claiming more land for white settlers.

As white people settled in nearby Minnesota, many Native Americans moved west to the Dakota Territory, looking for new homes. Other Native Americans tried to fight for their land. Several battles between Native Americans and the U.S. Army were fought in what is now the southern part of North Dakota.

By the late 1860s, the U.S. Army had won. The U.S. government then established **reservations**, or areas of land set aside for Native Americans. By 1870 the Dakota, Mandan, Hidatsa, and Arikara were living on reservations in the Dakota Territory.

Dakota women stand outside their homes near Fort Totten. Built by the U.S. government in 1867, Fort Totten and surrounding lands became the site of the Devils Lake Sioux (Dakota) Reservation.

Once the Native Americans were on reservations, railroad companies quickly built tracks across the Dakota Territory. Railroad companies wanted settlers to build homes and plant crops near the tracks. Then the settlers would buy train tickets when they needed to travel, and they would pay the railroads to ship crops to market.

One way railroad companies thought they could attract people was to help set up big, successful farms. In 1875 the Northern Pacific Railroad asked a man named Oliver Dalrymple to manage a 13,000-acre (5,300-hectare) wheat farm west of the city of Fargo. Dalrymple, known as the Minnesota Wheat King, accepted the offer and sold his wheat farm in Minnesota. In North Dakota, he did very well.

Bonanza farms required large numbers of workers, horses, and machinery.

Hearing of Dalrymple's success, other rich people set up even bigger wheat farms in North Dakota. Some were five times the size of Dalrymple's farm. Hundreds of men, horses, and machines were required to do all the work. Because these farms were so big and made so much money, they were called bonanza farms.

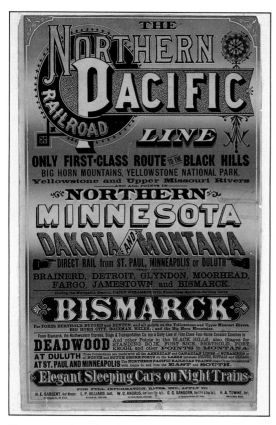

Posters advertised railroad service to the Dakota Territory.

The railroad companies were right. Stories of the bonanza farms attracted many people to eastern Dakota in the 1870s and 1880s. To attract even more settlers, the railroad companies went to northern Europe to advertise inexpensive farmland in the Dakota Territory. They also advertised in newspapers across the United States and in Canada.

In the 1880s, thousands of Norwegians and Germans came to the Dakota Territory. Many Canadians came to farm, too. So did people from New York, Minnesota, Wisconsin, and Iowa.

As the railroads laid tracks far-

Medora

One of North Dakota's most famous ranchers was a French nobleman, the Marquis de Mores. In 1883 the marquis came to North Dakota's Badlands with a new idea. Instead of sending North Dakota's cattle to be butchered in Eastern cities, the marquis wanted to butcher the cattle in North Dakota. The meat could then be shipped to market more easily than live cattle could.

To test his idea, the marquis built a town and named it after his wife, Medora. The marquis set up a ranch to raise cattle and sheep and to breed horses. He built a meat-packing plant, where the cattle would be butchered. The marquis also built a church and a school.

Many ranchers followed and Medora boomed. But the marquis didn't stay long. Drought and fire in 1886 killed the grass on which cattle depended for food. Thousands of cattle starved to death, and many ranchers in the area—including the marquis—gave up their operations. By 1889 Medora had been abandoned.

ther west, people followed to start ranches. Cowboys drove cattle into the Dakota Territory from faraway Colorado and Texas. Cattle thrived on the prairie grasses in western Dakota Territory.

Before long, however, too many cattle were grazing on the prairie, stripping it of its valuable grasses. The summer of 1886 was extremely hot and dry. Prairie fires destroyed even more grass.

By the time winter came, thousands of cattle were starving. Already very weak, many cows froze to death. Disappointed and penniless, some of the ranchers left the Dakota Territory.

But many people stayed. By the late 1800s, the Dakota Territory had more than 500,000 people—enough to apply for statehood. But

Because few trees grew in North Dakota, settlers didn't have much lumber for buildings. Instead, many people built their houses out of sod (blocks of dirt and grass).

The bald eagle on North Dakota's flag is a U.S. symbol of freedom. North Dakota's eagle grasps seven arrows and an olive branch with three red berries.

since most railroad tracks ran across the territory from east to west, people in the northern and southern parts of the Dakota Territory had little contact with each other. For that reason, the Dakota Territory was split in half. On November 2, 1889, North Dakota became the 39th state and South Dakota the 40th.

The Nonpartisan League

In the early 1900s, many of North Dakota's farmers were dissatisfied. The main offices of the railroads that carried North Dakota's crops to market were in Minnesota. So were the banks that lent money to North Dakota's farmers. The grain companies that bought North Dakota's wheat were also in Minnesota. North Dakota's farmers wanted more control. They wanted to have their own banks and their own grain companies.

In 1915 Arthur C. Townley, a North Dakota farmer, organized a group called the Nonpartisan League to help farmers. Townley traveled across the state talking to farmers about their problems. Farmers joined the league in large numbers, and by 1916 the league had 40,000 members and its own newspaper. With so many members, the league was very powerful. The league's leaders urged North Dakota's government to make changes to help the state's farmers. In 1919 the state government opened the Bank of North Dakota in Bismarck. By 1922 the state had opened its own grain elevator in Grand Forks, which stored grain at lower prices than the Minnesota elevators did. Both the bank and the elevator are still in operation today.

North Dakota's population grew quickly as railroads continued to build tracks in the state. Towns sprang up near the railroad tracks. In 1890 North Dakota had about 190,000 people. By 1910 more than 500,000 people lived in the state.

The 1920s were hard years for North Dakotans. Prices for crops were low. Little rain fell and crops did poorly. The price for wheat dropped still lower during the 1930s, and the dry weather continued. Grass didn't grow, so cattle starved. Dust storms blew away the dry topsoil, and huge swarms of grasshoppers ate almost everything that survived the **drought.**

A farmer looks to the sky, hoping that rain will come.

During World War II (1939–1945), economic conditions for North Dakota's farmers improved. Prices for crops and cattle were high because these products were needed to help feed U.S. troops. With better weather, crops were healthy and farmers made a lot of money.

In 1946, after terrible floods along the Missouri River, North Dakotans began building the Garrison Dam. The dam, which took 14 years to build, prevents floods by holding excess rainwater in an artificial lake. Water from the lake is then released in powerful streams that turn engines. These engines create electricity for homes and businesses in North Dakota.

The U.S. government created many jobs in 1957 when it built an air-force base in Minot, North Dakota. In 1960 a second base, in Grand Forks, was completed. These bases train pilots and shelter bombers and nuclear missiles.

More jobs and money came to North Dakota with the discovery of oil in the western part of the state. By the 1970s, oil had become an important industry. Many North Dakotans earned money by pumping and refining this energy-producing mineral.

When the Garrison Dam was built in the 1940s, 155,000 acres (62,775 hectares) of farmland that belonged to the Mandan, Hidatsa, and Arikara were plunged under water.

8,000 B.C.   **400 B.C.**   **A.D. 1000**   **1738**   **1804**   **1812**

Native Americans come to the region now called North Dakota

Woodland Indians settle in eastern North Dakota

Mandan Indians settle along the Missouri River

La Vérendrye visits North Dakota

Lewis and Clark build Fort Mandan

Thomas Douglas brings immigrants to Pembina

A statue of a buffalo stands on the grounds of North Dakota's capitol, a skyscraper in Bismarck.

1861 — Dakota Territory is established

1875 — Oliver Dalrymple starts first bonanza farm

1889 — North Dakota becomes the 39th state

1946 — Construction of Garrison Dam begins

1957 — Air-force base is built at Minot

1988 — Vision 2000 Committee is formed

North Dakotans, however, still rely mostly on agriculture to make a living. Since earnings from farms are very unpredictable, North Dakotans are looking for ways to bring different kinds of jobs to the state. In 1988 North Dakota's leaders formed the Vision 2000 Committee and held meetings across the state to get ideas from citizens. In this way, North Dakotans are working together to provide good living conditions for everyone in their state.

Living and Working in North Dakota

When pioneers came to North Dakota, they came to farm the rich prairie soil or to graze cattle on the western plains. More than 100 years later, about half of North Dakota's 638,800 residents still live on farms or in small towns.

Only four cities have more than 25,000 people. About 74,000 people live in Fargo, the largest city. Bismarck is the state capital. Grand Forks is home to the University of North Dakota, and Minot is the site of an air-force base.

Many North Dakotans have European ancestors.

Most North Dakotans were born in the United States. Close to 95 percent of the state's people are descendants of European settlers who came in the 1800s. Their ancestors came from Norway and Germany, as well as Canada. Native Americans, Hispanics, African Americans, and Asians make up the rest of the state's population.

North Dakotans have often looked to their own people for en-

44

tertainment. The state has many community theater groups, including the Little Country Theater in Fargo. Minot, Fargo, and Grand Forks each sponsor a symphony orchestra.

Every Memorial Day weekend, the town of Medora holds the Dakota Cowboy Poetry Gathering, where cowboy poets from around the country recite their verses. In August the town of Sentinel Butte holds the Champions' Ride Rodeo. The Mandan, the Hidatsa, the Arikara, the Ojibway, and the Dakota celebrate their heritage at the United Tribes Powwow, held each September in Bismarck.

These young North Dakotans play at the Devils Lake Sioux Reservation.

North Dakota has no professional sports teams. But the University of North Dakota's hockey team, the Fighting Sioux, has won five national championships. The Bison, the football team at North Dakota State University, have won eight national championships.

The hockey team at the University of North Dakota *(above)* and the football team at North Dakota State University *(right)* have each won several national championships.

Canoeists paddle on the Cannonball River.

Throughout the year, North Dakotans enjoy the outdoors. They go boating and fishing on Devils Lake or Lake Sakakawea. Many people picnic and camp at Lake Metigoshe State Park, one of North Dakota's 12 state parks. Animal lovers watch eagles, antelope, and bison in Theodore Roosevelt National Park.

47

Flax is grown for its seeds and for its fiber, which is used to make linen.

North Dakota earns more money from agriculture than most other states do. The state has close to 30,000 farms and ranches. About 90 percent of North Dakota's land is used either for grazing cattle or for growing crops.

Wheat is North Dakota's major crop. In fact, only Kansas grows more wheat than North Dakota. Some of North Dakota's farmers plant a special variety of wheat called durum. Durum wheat is used to make spaghetti and other pastas.

North Dakota's farmers plant many other crops as well. The state ranks first in growing barley, sunflowers, and flax. Linseed oil, which is used to make paint, comes from crushed flaxseeds. Oats, rye, and sugar beets are also important crops in the state.

Many North Dakotans make a living from raising wheat *(above)* **and cattle** *(inset).*

North Dakota's farmers grow hay to feed the state's cattle. Ranchers raise beef and dairy cattle. Because hogs like to eat corn, most pigs are found on farms in the eastern part of the state, where corn grows well. North Dakotans also raise sheep and poultry.

About three-fourths of North Dakota's workers have jobs that provide a service to others. The people who sell equipment to farmers have service jobs. So do the bankers who help farmers get loans. Some service workers have jobs in restaurants and government offices. The people who work at the air-force bases in Minot and Grand Forks have service jobs, too.

Waiters in Bismarck are among the many service workers in North Dakota.

50

Two soldiers meet while on patrol at the air-force base in Minot.

North Dakota has few manufacturing jobs because many companies can't afford the high cost of transporting goods from the state to markets in distant cities. Most of the 15,000 North Dakotans who have manufacturing jobs process food from the crops and livestock that farmers provide. Workers at plants in Dickinson and Finley make frozen bread dough. Many people have jobs at meat-packing plants in Fargo. Sugar is processed from sugar beets at refineries in Grand Forks, Hillsboro, and Wahpeton.

Billions of tons of coal lie under the ground in western North Dakota.

Oil, which was discovered in North Dakota in 1951, earns the state more money than any other mineral.

Some North Dakotans make a living by taking minerals from the earth. Oil is pumped from underground oil fields in western North Dakota. Later it is cleaned and processed into gasoline at an oil refinery in Mandan in the southern part of the state.

Other miners dig the state's deposits of coal, some of which are found in the Badlands. The coal is then burned at power plants to produce electricity. North Dakotans also dig for clay, which is used to make bricks and ceramics. Road construction crews depend upon the state's sand and gravel to build roads.

Potholes make good nesting sites for ducks and geese.

Protecting the Environment

North Dakota's wetlands—which include pot-holes, bogs, marshes, swamps, and the shorelines of rivers and lakes—provide food, water, and shelter for many animals and plants. Salamanders and frogs live in wetlands. Plants that need lots of water, such as the prairie fringed orchid and the marsh fern, grow in wetlands.

Muskrats dig their burrows into the banks of streams. A small, sand-colored bird called the piping plover makes its nest on the sandbars of the Missouri River. In the spring, between two and three million ducklings hatch in North Dakota's potholes.

Prairie fringed orchid

55

But potholes and other wetlands in North Dakota are disappearing. More than half of the state's original wetlands are now gone. Farmers drain wetlands or fill them up with dirt to create more land for growing crops. Workers drain wetlands in places where they need more solid ground for building roads, houses, and stores.

As North Dakota's wetlands vanish, so do plants and animals. Plants that need marshy areas to survive die when their watery habitats, or homes, are drained. Animals lose safe places to make their homes. Wetland grasses, for example, offer protection for ducks and their chicks. When a duck's wetland nesting site disappears, the duck is forced to move to an area where it may not be safe from predators such as foxes.

Wetlands offer more than a safe place for animals to make their homes. North Dakota's potholes, for example, help control pollution. After a heavy rain, harmful chemicals that people use to kill weeds and insects sometimes wash into potholes. Water in potholes moves slowly, so the chemicals have time to settle to the bottom. This makes the water that runs out of the potholes and into nearby lakes and streams less polluted.

Ducks *(inset)* **find food and water in North Dakota's wildlife refuges** *(above)* — **areas set aside for plants and animals to live undisturbed by humans.**

Dry potholes fill up with rainwater after storms, helping to prevent nearby rivers from flooding.

Potholes also act as dams that control floods. When heavy rain falls, or when snow melts in the spring, potholes fill up and hold this water. The water then trickles away slowly or eventually dries up. Because the potholes hold extra water, nearby streams and rivers are less likely to overflow and flood the surrounding land.

The people of North Dakota are finding ways to save their wetlands. In 1987 the state passed a law requiring landowners who plan to drain 80 acres (32 hectares) or more of wetlands to apply for a permit from the state. If the permit is granted, the landowner may drain the wetlands but must also help pay to replace the same amount of wetlands elsewhere in the state. This way, North Dakota will not lose any more of its valuable wetlands.

MIGRATORY BIRD HUNTING AND CONSERVATION STAMP
$15
VOID AFTER JUNE 30, 1992
King Eiders
U. S. DEPARTMENT OF THE INTERIOR

Instead of draining potholes, some farmers plant around them ***(above).*** **And when hunters buy the duck stamp** ***(inset)*** **for their hunting license, some of the money goes to preserve North Dakota's wetlands.**

North Dakota and the U.S. government are also working together to save the wetlands. In some cases, the U.S. government buys wetlands and the surrounding land to make sure private owners do not drain or fill them. In other cases, the U.S. government pays North Dakota's farmers to leave wetlands alone when they are filled with water. During dry periods, farmers may plant crops or graze cattle in the dry wetlands.

When North Dakotans want to go duck hunting, they must first buy a license and two stamps. One of these stamps is called the duck stamp. The money that hunters pay for this stamp goes toward protecting wetlands in North Dakota and across the country.

The other stamp is called the habitat stamp. Some of the money from this stamp is used to preserve the habitats—including wetlands—of North Dakota's wildlife. With careful planning, humans as well as plant and animal life in North Dakota will benefit from the wetlands for many years to come.

North Dakota's Famous People

ACTORS & ENTERTAINERS

▲ PHYLLIS FRELICH

Angie Dickinson (born 1931) grew up in Edgeley, North Dakota. In the 1970s, she starred in the TV series "Police Woman." Dickinson has also been in many movies, including *Dressed to Kill* and *Charlie Chan and the Curse of the Dragon Queen*.

▲ ANGIE DICKINSON

Phyllis Frelich (born 1944), a deaf actress, was one of the founding members of the National Theater of the Deaf. She has appeared in many plays, including the popular Broadway production of *Children of a Lesser God*, for which she won a Tony Award. Frelich is from Devils Lake, North Dakota.

Dorothy Stickney (born 1903) is known for her role in the Broadway play *Life With Father*, in which she co-starred from 1939 to 1943. Stickney also appeared in the 1971 pilot for the TV show "The Waltons." She is from Dickinson, North Dakota.

DOROTHY STICKNEY ▶

ARTISTS

◀ RICHARD EDLUND

Richard Edlund (born 1940) of Fargo is a special-effects technician. His work appears in several films, including *Poltergeist*, *Ghostbusters*, and *Fright Night*. Edlund has won six Academy Awards.

James Rosenquist (born 1933) is famous for a painting of a U.S. bomber plane. Entitled *F-1-11*, the painting is actually larger than the plane itself. Rosenquist is from Grand Forks.

ATHLETES

Virgil Hill (born 1963), a boxer, grew up in Grand Forks. Hill has won the Golden Gloves and the North American boxing titles, as well as a silver medal in the 1984 Olympic Games. In 1987 he won the World Boxing Association's light heavyweight title, which he defended until 1990.

Roger Maris (1934–1985), a baseball player for the New York Yankees, grew up in Fargo. Maris was the American League's Most Valuable Player in 1960 and 1961. By hitting his 61st home run in 1961, Maris broke the record for the most home runs hit in one season.

▼ ROGER MARIS

▲ VIRGIL HILL

▲ JAMES BUCHLI

EXPLORERS

James Buchli (born 1945) is an astronaut who has been a crew member on several space voyages. In 1985 he was a flight engineer on the *Discovery* satellite-launching mission. That same year, Buchli was part of the *Challenger* crew for a Spacelab mission. In 1989 he again flew with *Discovery*. Buchli grew up in Fargo.

Sakakawea (1786?–1812), a Shoshone Indian woman, was captured by Hidatsa Indians as a child. She later married a French Canadian trader named Toussaint Charbonneau. Sakakawea, also known as Sacagawea, and her husband accompanied the Lewis and Clark expedition west from North Dakota, helping as guides and interpreters.

63

▼ RONALD DAVIES

▲ HAROLD SCHAFER

Ronald Davies (born 1904), a judge from Grand Forks, became famous when called to fill in for a federal judge in Little Rock, Arkansas, in 1957. Davies's first task in Arkansas was to enforce the famous U.S. Supreme Court decision to allow black students and white students to attend the same public schools.

Harold Schafer (born 1912) of Stanton, North Dakota, became a big name in the floor-wax industry. In 1942 he established the Gold Seal Company and eventually developed it into a multi-million-dollar international business.

MUSICIANS

Lynn Anderson (born 1947) is a country-western singer who recorded such hit songs as "Rose Garden" and "Top of the World," which became popular in the 1970s. Anderson is originally from Grand Forks.

Peggy Lee (born 1920) is from Jamestown, North Dakota. As a singer, she toured with Benny Goodman's band, going on to record with stars such as Bing Crosby and Jimmy Durante. Lee worked on the music for the film *Lady and the Tramp* and starred in two motion pictures—*The Jazz Singer* and *Pete Kelly's Blues.*

Lawrence Welk (1903–1992) was from Strasburg, North Dakota. Welk formed a band in the 1920s and became popular in the 1950s as the bandleader and host of TV's "The Lawrence Welk Show." Welk was known as the King of Champagne Music.

▲ PEGGY LEE

LAWRENCE
▼ WELK

64

LOUIS L'AMOUR ▶

◀ **LOUISE ERDRICH**

Louise Erdrich (born 1954) is a poet and the author of several short stories and books. Erdrich and her husband, author Michael Dorris, wrote *The Crown of Columbus,* a novel about the search for the lost journal of Christopher Columbus. Erdrich grew up in Wahpeton, North Dakota, and is a member of the Turtle Mountain Band of Chippewa.

Louis L'Amour (1908–1988) wrote more million-copy bestsellers than any other American writer of fiction. His many action-packed novels, short stories, and film and television scripts are known for their realistic descriptions of life in the Old West. L'Amour was born in Jamestown, North Dakota.

◀ **ERIC SEVAREID**

ERA BELL ▶ THOMPSON

Eric Sevareid (born 1912) began his journalism career as a newspaper reporter and went on to become one of the most well-known faces of television news. Born in Velva, North Dakota, Sevareid was a news correspondent for CBS during World War II and later appeared regularly on the CBS Evening News.

Era Bell Thompson (1905–1987) moved to Driscoll, North Dakota, with her family as a child. Thompson studied at the University of North Dakota and went on to publish several books. In 1947 she joined *Ebony* magazine, for which she became the international editor.

65

Facts-at-a-Glance

Nickname: Flickertail State
Song: "North Dakota Hymn"
Motto: Liberty and Union, Now and Forever, One and Inseparable
Flower: wild prairie rose
Tree: American elm
Bird: western meadowlark

Population: 638,800*
Rank in population, nationwide: 47th
Area: 70,704 sq mi (183,123 sq km)
Rank in area, nationwide: 19th
Date and ranking of statehood:
    November 2,1889, the 39th state
Capital: Bismarck
Major Cities (and populations*):
    Fargo (74,111), Grand Forks (49,425),
    Bismarck (49,256), Minot (34,544),
    Dickinson (16,097)
U.S. senators: 2
U.S. representatives: 1
Electoral votes: 3

Places to visit: Bonanzaville, USA, in West Fargo, Chateau de Mores near Medora, Knife River Indian Villages National Historic Site near Stanton, Theodore Roosevelt National Park near Medora, Writing Rock near Grenora

Annual events: Winterfest in Minot (Feb.), Fort Seward Wagon Train in Jamestown (June), Rough Rider Days in Dickinson (July), Potato Bowl in Grand Forks (Sept.), Norsk Hostefest in Minot (Oct.)

*1990 census

66

Natural resources: soil, petroleum, natural gas, lignite coal, sand and gravel, clay, salt

Agricultural products: wheat, beef, barley, hay, sunflower seeds, milk, sugar beets, flaxseed, oats, rye, potatoes

Manufactured goods: food products, machinery, petroleum products, printed materials, transportation equipment

ENDANGERED SPECIES
Mammals—northern swift fox, black bear, fisher, black-footed ferret, river otter
Birds—white-winged scoter, common merganser, bald eagle, peregrine falcon, merlin, sandhill crane, least tern
Fish—pallid sturgeon
Plants—prairie milkweed, frostweed, pinweed, St. John's-wort, moonwort, leathery grape fern, prairie fringed orchid, pull-up muhly, ricegrass, Dakota buckwheat, yellow monkey flower

WHERE NORTH DAKOTANS WORK
Services—53 percent
　(services includes jobs in trade; community, social, & personal services; finance, insurance & real estate; transportation, communication, & utilities)
Government—22 percent
Agriculture—14 percent
Manufacturing —5 percent
Construction—4 percent
Mining—2 percent

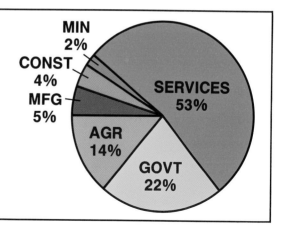

PRONUNCIATION GUIDE

Agassiz (AG-uh-see)

Arikara (uh-RIHK-uh-ruh)

Dalrymple, Oliver
(duhl-RIHM-puhl, AHL-uh-vuhr)

Hidatsa (hih-DAHT-suh)

La Vérendrye, Pierre de
(lah vay-rahn-DREE, pee-AIR duh)

Mandan (MAN-dan)

Minot (MY-naht)

Pembina (PEHM-buh-nuh)

Sakakawea (sak-ak-uh-WEE-uh)

Sheyenne (shy-EHN)

Sioux (SOO)

Wahpeton (WAW-puh-tuhn)

Glossary

butte   An isolated hill or mountain with steep sides.

drift   A mixture of clay, sand, and gravel deposited by a glacier, plus any materials added to this mixture by the running water of a melting glacier. Areas where drift has been deposited have very good soil for farming.

drought   A long period of extreme dryness due to lack of rain or snow.

glacier   A large body of ice and snow that moves slowly over land.

ice age   A period when ice sheets cover large regions of the earth. The term *Ice Age* usually refers to the most recent one, called the Pleistocene, which began almost 2 million years ago and ended about 10,000 years ago.

immigrant   A person who moves into a foreign country and settles there.

plateau   A large, relatively flat area that stands above the surrounding land.

pothole   A small depression in the land. After a rainstorm or when nearby snow melts, potholes fill up with water. In periods of hot and dry weather, the potholes often dry up.

prairie   A large area of level or gently rolling grassy land with few trees.

precipitation   Rain, snow, and other forms of moisture.

reservation   Public land set aside by the government to be used by Native Americans.

Index

Acknowledgments:

Maryland Cartographics, pp. 2, 11; William J. Weber/Visuals Unlimited, pp. 2-3; © Kirtley-Perkins/Visuals Unlimited, p. 58; Independent Picture Service, pp. 6, 21, 22; Jack Lindstrom, p. 7; Craig Bihrle, North Dakota Game and Fish Department, pp. 8-9, 14, 17, 52, 53, 57 (inset); © Craig Bihrle, p. 49 (inset); Kent and Donna Dannen, pp. 10, 54; Lynda Richards, pp. 12, 13, 43, 48, 49, 57; State Historical Society of North Dakota, pp. 23, 25, 26, 29, 30-31, 32, 33, 34, 36, 37, 63 (top left), 64 (top right), 65 (top right and bottom right); Library of Congress, p. 27; Jeff Greenberg, pp. 39, 40, 45, 47, 50, 68; Betty A. Kubis/Root Resources, p. 42; Cary Sukut, p. 44, 71; C.W. Pack Sports, p. 46 (top left); Dana Sherman, p. 46 (bottom right); U.S. Air Force photo, p. 51; Linda Huhn, p. 55; Annie Griffiths Belt, p. 60; USFWS, Federal Duck Stamp Office, p. 60 (inset); Hollywood Book and Poster, Inc., pp. 62 (center left), 64 (bottom left); NDIRS-NDSU, Fargo, pp. 62 (top right and center right), 64 (top left and bottom right), 65 (bottom left); Boss Film Studios, p. 62 (bottom); NASA, p. 63 (bottom); National Baseball Hall of Fame and Museum, Inc., p. 63 (top right); Michael Dorris, p. 65 (top left); Jean Matheny, p. 66.